The Miracles of Jesus and the Miracles of the Early Hebrew Prophets

The Miracles of Jesus and the Miracles of the Early Hebrew Prophets

Rabbi Herbert M. Baumgard D.H.L., D.D.

*Publication of this book would not have been
possible without the support of*

Daniel and Lori Baumgard

Copyright @ 2013
The Miracles of Jesus and the Miracles
of the Early Hebrew Prophets

ISBN 9781602802742

**Distributed by
KTAV Publishing House, Inc.**
527 Empire Blvd.
Brooklyn, NY 11225
www.ktav.com
orders@ktav.com
Tel. (718) 972-5449
Fax (718)-972-6307

Dedication

This book is dedicated to my dear wife of sixty-three years, Selma, who passed away on February 1, 2012.

Sharing the dedication are the children of our marriage, Dr. Jonathan Baumgard (and his wife Wendy), Daniel Baumgard (and his wife Lori) and Shira Baumgard Garvett (and her husband Fred). All of these people have been sources of affection while encouraging me to produce this book.

Acknowledgements

Many are those to whom thanks are due for help in the writing of or the preparation of this book. These include Anita Marks, my secretary, who bore with me through the experimental phases of the book. Susan Carney made suggestions after pre-reading the early text.

Table of Contents

Preface 15

Chapter 1:
Similarities Between Jesus and Elijah-Elisha 17

Chapter 2:
Comparisons to Jeremiah 25

Chapter 3:
The Book of Isaiah 37

Chapter 4:
The "Individual" Who Suffers in Isaiah 53 41

Chapter 5:
The Book of Daniel 43

Chapter 6:
The Jewishness of Jesus 47

Chapter 7:
The Pharisees 51

Chapter 8:
Understanding Jesus 55

Chapter 9:
The Son of God 59

Chapter 10:
The Crucifixion 63

Chapter 11:
Which Messiah? 67

Chapter 12:
The Allegory of Jonah and the Whale 77

Chapter 13:
Anti-Jewish Sentiments in the New Testament 79

Chapter 14:
A Curious Event in the Life of Jesus 83

Chapter 15:
Should Jews Read the New Testament? 87

Glossary 95

Bibliography 96

Preface

Many books have been written on the subject of Jesus, but no one, to this author's knowledge, has undertaken a detailed comparison of the major events in the life of Jesus with earlier events in the lives of the Hebrew prophets who lived long before Jesus.

Our book attempts to fill this void.

A review of the miracles performed by the prophets Elijah and Elisha, for example, shows a remarkable likeness to later events attributed to Jesus.[1] Some readers may find this similarity to be unusual, but this author sees the echo of older happenings in another light. After all, Jesus was a Jew who was immersed in his people's teachings and history. Nothing reveals that identity more than the memory he applies to situations that he encounters in his lifetime.

Our book attempts to illustrate many of these similarities. It is this author's hope that this revelation will bring modern Jews and Christians closer together.

A sub-question this book considers is: "Should Jews read the New Testament?" The author attempts to show why his answer is in the affirmative.

---

1. A Christian Bible professor of mine at the Union Theological Seminary in New York City called these earlier events "Foreshadowings."

Chapter One

Similarities Between Jesus and Elijah-Elisha

The more this author reads the New Testament, the more he becomes convinced that much (not all) of the description of the life of Jesus is composed by the retelling of events in the Hebrew Scriptures, with Jesus as the hero replacing the hero in the Hebrew Scriptures.

This view is supported by comparing some of the stories told about the Hebrew prophets, Elijah and Elisha with some of the stories told about Jesus. You, perhaps, know that in most ancient times, many peoples of the Middle East had seers or soothsayers who were pictured as being miracle workers and foretellers of the future. Part of the genius of the Hebrews is that they slowly developed a new kind of religious figure out of the seer. Certainly, by the year 600 BCE, the seer seldom appears in the culture of Israel. In his place is the prophet. The prophet of this period has ceased to be a miracle worker.[2] Even his ability to foretell specific events in

---

2. Dr. Harry M. Orlinsky has written on this theme. See his essay on "The Seer-Priest and the Prophet in Ancient Israel", pp. 39ff, *Essays in Biblical Culture and Bible Foundation*, KTAV Publishing House Inc., New York, 1974

the future has been minimized. Instead, the Prophet appears as a moral interpreter of history, as one who offers specific predictions which are valid, if certain kinds of indifference to the poor continue, and if the basic Hebrew code of laws is not followed. True, the magnificent "Literary Prophets" of Israel, like Amos, Hosea, Jeremiah and Isaiah, speak as if they are proclaiming the living commands of God Himself, but they eschew magic. They are not concerned with making rods turn into snakes, nor are they concerned with turning aside the waters so that they can walk on dry land. Instead, Amos proclaims, "…Let justice roll down as the mighty waters and righteousness like an unfailing stream,"[3] and Jeremiah inveighs against the hypocrisy of Temple ritual while those in power are insensitive to the suffering of the mass of people.

The moralistic Prophets of the Hebrews, preachers of internationalism and universalism, did not suddenly appear among the Jews. They are the end product of a slow and steady development. The prophets about whom we speak primarily now, Elijah and Elisha, were only the early prototypes of the later "Literary Prophets."[4] While these two men, Elijah and Elisha, also spoke of justice, they combined their moralistic teachings with the working of miracles. Indeed, they belonged to an age where the people insisted upon the performance of some magic from a "Man of God," before he could be accepted as one who taught the divine message.

It seems to this author that Jesus, who lived perhaps 600-800 years after Elijah and Elisha, had a great deal in common with this kind of earlier prophet. While Jesus quotes Jeremiah

3. Martin L. King quotes the Hebrew Prophet Amos in his wonderful speech in Washington. Many people think this teaching originated with King. See Amos 5:24.

4. Note that we distinguish between the miracle-working prophets and the later Literary Prophets by spelling the designation of the latter as Prophet. Elijah and Elisha appear in the 9th century B.C.E.

who lived 600 years before him, and while he quotes Isaiah, who belongs to a like period of Jewish history, nonetheless, Jesus appears in the New Testament more in the mould of the earlier Elijah, than like Jeremiah or Isaiah.

What is the evidence of this thesis? The New Testament presents Jesus as a unique figure because, among other things, he heals the sick, he performs miracles like walking on the water, and he rises from the dead. Jeremiah and Isaiah, among the later Literary Prophets did not pretend to do any of these things. Perhaps they represent a more sophisticated era of Hebraic history; but Elijah and Elisha, as we shall see, were precisely this kind of figure, and it seems that some of the Jesus stories seem to be but a re-telling of some of the earlier Elijah-Elisha stories.

Our source is the book of Matthew, designated by some scholars as the first of the New Testament books. In the eighth chapter of Matthew, we are told that Jesus heals a leper of his disease (vv. 1-4). In the ninth chapter a paralytic is enabled, according to the text, to rise up from his bed (vv. 1-8). Also, in this chapter, a blind man is enabled to see (vv. 27-30). These things are described in the New Testament as part of the evidence that Jesus is greater than a man, indeed, that he is divine. Elijah and Elisha, early Old Testament prophets, do this type of thing in an earlier time. Still the "Hebrew Scriptures" does not make a claim that these men are divine. For example, in the second book of Kings, chapter five (vv. 1-14), we are told that the King of Syria writes the King of Israel and asks that he help to cure a certain Syrian, named Naaman, of his leprosy. The King of Israel rends his clothes in despair and says, (v. 7), "Am I God to kill and make alive?" The prophet Elisha, however, is not at all dismayed at this request. He sent a messenger to the Hebrew King saying (v. 8), "Why have you rent your clothes? Let him (i.e., the Syrian) come to me, that he may know that there is a prophet in Israel." In other words, Elisha clearly considered it to be one of his ordinary functions as a prophet to heal people of leprosy. The text then recounts how Elisha cures Naaman, who happens to be a captain in the Syrian army. The cure is described as being miraculous in nature.

In the fourth chapter of the second book of Kings, we are told that a woman from Shunam comes to Elisha and complains that her son has died. We are told that Elisha brings the boy back to life (4:32-37). A similar incident is ascribed to Elijah (1 Kings 17:17-24). Indeed, we are told that contact with a prophet was so vital that when a dead man was thrown into Elisha's grave, he was returned to life by contact with the bones of the deceased prophet (2 Kings 13:21). In spite of this apparent ability to work miracles, these prophets were never deemed to be more than mortal by the ancient Hebrews. Whatever they did, it was believed, was by virtue of a special gift of God to them. The woman, whose son Elijah brings to life, merely says, "Now I know you are a man of God…" (1 Kings 17:24).

One of the great miracles claimed for Jesus is that of walking on the water, something his disciples thought no mortal could do. In the eighth chapter of the book of Matthew, we are told that Jesus was in a boat with his disciples when a great storm arose. His disciples were fearful, but we are told that Jesus arose, "and rebuked the winds and the sea; and there was a great calm." The New Testament continues, "and the men marveled, saying, "What sort of man is this, that even winds and sea obey him?" (8: 23-27). The story occurs again, slightly varied (14:25), and in this second situation, Jesus is described as actually walking on the water.

The story concludes that when the disciples got into the boat, they worshipped him, saying (v. 33) "truly, you are the Son of God."[5]

In the second book of Kings, the second chapter, (v.8), we are told that with fifty of his disciples watching, Elijah took his mantle and parted the waters of the River Jordan and walked on the dry land with Elisha at his side. Later (2:14), we are told that Elisha performs the same miracle. He, too, parts the water and walks on the dry land.

In the fifteenth chapter of the book of Matthew (v. 32ff) we are told that Jesus took a few loaves of bread and fed a crowd of four thousand people. This, too, is taken to be a sign of his special nature. How could so many be fed with so little? In the Hebrew Scriptures, Elisha feeds a large group of people with just a few loaves (2 Kings 4:42-44). In almost an identical situation, and in another story, a woman with only one jar of oil, on command of the prophet Elisha, pours from this one jar of oil endlessly filling many more jars of oil to sell for money, while the first jar is never diminished (2 Kings 4:1ff). The object of all these stories is to teach that where there is love and faith, much can be done with very little. See also where Elijah is fed by the woman who has no food (1 Kings 17:8-16)!

The New Testament tells us that while Jesus seems to die, he was seen to be resurrected on the third day. To be sure, the Hebrew Scriptures does not speak of either Elijah or Elisha being resurrected. Elisha, the younger of the two, apparently dies a normal death, although, as we have described, his very bones seemed to have the power to bring another dead person back to life (2 Kings 13:21).

---

5. See now a "man of God," said of Elisha, (1 Kings 17:24) but note that When Elisha succeeds Elijah, students of the prophets bowed down before Elisha (2 Kings 2:15).

What happens to Elijah? To be sure, he is not resurrected, but neither does he die, according to the biblical text! The text tells us that Elijah is gathered up to heaven by the whirlwind, (2 Kings 2:11). He is the only figure in the Jewish Scripture who does not die a natural death, and Jewish tradition says that one day Elijah will return to earth, in advance of a continuing day of peace and good will, i.e., ushering in the Messiah. Although Elijah merely disappears and does not seem to die, he is not said to be divine. Whatever happened to him, we are led to believe, was merely what God had ordained for one of his human messengers.

The conclusion of all this is that Jesus is in the mould of great Jewish figures that lived before him. His teachings, in many cases, are quotations from Jewish scripture or other Jewish sources in the Talmud. His miracle-working is largely a restatement of stories told about Elijah and Elisha who lived 800 years before him. The interesting point for us is that after Elisha, the Hebrew people substantially seemed to outgrow this earlier tradition of the miracle worker and developed what some Jewish scholars consider to be a higher type of religious personality, in the later "Literary Prophets." These prophets are each identified with a book that bears his name. These later Prophets were unique in their zeal for the cause of the people, but they are not described as performing miraculous events. If it were not for the fact that the New Testament suggests that Jesus is divine, we could place him, at least in part, as a Jewish figure comparable on the one hand to Elijah and Elisha, and on the other, to Jeremiah.[6]

---

6 In the "New Testament," Jesus is described as standing in the Temple court and declaring in the name of God, "Has my house become a den of robbers unto you?" (Mark 11:15-19 and Luke 19:46). These are the exact words proclaimed by the Prophet Jeremiah in the similar situation 600 years earlier (Jer. 7: 9-11).

If we ask how it is that Jesus did not seek to present himself entirely in the image of the later Prophets like Jeremiah, we have to try to understand the times in which Jesus lived, and the region in which he apparently grew up and preached. He was apparently reared in that part of Israel in which Elijah and Elisha had served. The New Testament tells us that although Jesus was born in the more sophisticated southern region of Judea, he apparently lived and taught in the northern region near Galilee and near the Syrian border. It was precisely here that the Elijah-Elisha legends had their greatest rootage in the Jewish people, and it is possible that Jesus was the heir to this older and less urbanized version of Judaism. Further, Jesus lived in a time when many Jews, because of the cruelty of their Roman conquerors, despaired of the usefulness of a rationalistic religion and looked for a sudden miracle to save them. These Jews would likely be drawn to the image of a miracle-working prophet.

According to some scholars, Christian as well as Jewish, it was not until long after the death of Jesus that his Elijah-type personality was merged with the image of a "Son of God" coming in the sky to judge between the righteous and the wicked. This last concept was Persian in origin and repeated in the book of Daniel.[7]

---

7. See our discussion in Chapter 4, The Book of Daniel.

Chapter Two

Comparisons to Jeremiah

The book of Matthew in the New Testament tells us that when Jesus came to Jerusalem, by way of the Mt. of Olives and riding on a white donkey, all the people were stirred and said, "This is the prophet Jesus from Nazareth"[8] (21:1-11).

We can see revealed in the pages of the New Testament evidence of the sharp battles between different Jewish groups of that period such as the Pharisees, the Sadducees, the Zealots and the apocalyptic preachers.[9] There is also revealed the battle between the ruling power, the Romans, and the Judeans who were suffering under the Roman conquest. As the story unfolds in the New Testament, Jesus appears as the foe of all of these groups, except the apocalyptic preachers.

---

8. In "Ancient Judaism and The New Testament," Macmillan Co., N.Y., 1959. Dr. F.C. Grant holds that Jesus looked upon himself as a prophet, p. 81ff.

9. See *Who Crucified Jesus.*, S. Zeitlin, 2nd ed. Harper, N.Y., 1947 p. 96ff on the Apocalyptic Pharisees. Of lesser size were the Zealots who culled their participants from the other groups. The Essenes isolated themselves from these groups away from Jerusalem and in the desert area (Masada).

While he seems to identify with the suffering of the prophets who came before him, and while Jesus quotes many of the prophets at great length, his great hero seems to be John the Baptist. John was a Jew who believed with a few other evangelical teachers that God was about to bring about the cataclysmic upheaval which would result in a purification of the world. In this upheaval, nations and multitudes would be destroyed; those who are evil would be consigned to suffering, and the righteous would be rewarded. John went about teaching, "repent for the kingdom of heaven is at hand." John and his followers believed that the great upheaval was imminent and the more glorious reign of God, the reign of justice and peace, was around the corner. As a sign of repentance, John required his followers to practice *t'vilah*, that is, to be baptized with water; hence, he was called, "John the Baptist."

The New Testament tells us that Jesus came to John to be baptized. From this we learn that Jesus annexed himself to the apocalyptic group. Jesus, we are told, apparently decided to become the leader of the sect which John the Baptist had dominated before him. Indeed, Jesus is quoted as saying that John was Elijah returned to the earth to announce the coming of the Messiah, namely, Jesus (Matt 11:14). The followers of Jesus, like the followers of John, were those most ready to believe a doctrine which taught that "the last shall be first." The message of Jesus was geared to the poor and to the lower classes. Perhaps that is why Jesus spoke in parables or stories; that is why Jesus inveighed against the rich; that is why he seemed to be against all aspects of the establishment, whether it be the Roman government or the Jewish aristocracy. Jesus himself was a Pharisee, but he was critical of those Pharisees who overly displayed their "righteousness." On the basis of his teachings and his attitude, many scholars conclude that Jesus was himself a Pharisee, drawing his teachings from a tradition followed by the Pharisees. The Sadducees were the wealthy quislings assimilated into the Roman culture and governing group. The Sadducees and the apocalyptic group were diametrically opposed to one another. They had little communication. The Pharisees and the apocalyptic group were engaged in a struggle to influence the mind of the masses.[10]

Was Jesus a prophet? Can we claim him, no more or less, as a grand and fervent proclaimer of truth and friend of the poor and powerless, as was Micah or Jeremiah? The answer is not so simple. A prophet in the Jewish tradition was a "*Navi*," that is, one who helped to bring to pass that which God wanted.[11] The great "Literary Prophets," men like Isaiah, Amos and Jeremiah, were men who either possessed, or were thought to possess, direct power from God. The Book of Jeremiah quotes God as saying to Jeremiah, "See, I have set you this day over nations and over kingdoms, to pluck up and to break down, to destroy and to overthrow, to build and to plant" (Jer 1:10). When the prophet spoke, our ancestors believed, it was impossible to stay the realization of that which he had declared, whether it was favorable or unfavorable. The prophet mediated the command of God, and once the command (*davar*-word) was vocalized, nothing could stay that event from taking place. Yet, with all of this power, or assumed power, none of the prophets ever thought that he was more than a vessel for God's spirit. No prophet ever dreamed that he was more than human, more than a mere conveyor of God's message.

At some places in the New Testament, Jesus seems to say

---

10. See G.F. Moore on the Pharisee in "Judaism." Vol. 1, p. 67ff, Cambridge, Harvard University Press, 1950, 6th Impression.

11. Most authorities translate *Navi*, "one who proclaims, speaks." I hold with those who believe that the title is more dynamic, coming from the verb "to bring", i.e., to mediate the divine word or proclamation (*davar*).

that he regards himself in a similar way. For example, he is quoted as saying, "Not everyone who calls me Lord shall enter the Kingdom of Heaven, but he who does the will of my Father who is in Heaven" (Matt 7:21ff); but in other passages Jesus seems to say that he is to be identified with God Himself (Matt 22:41ff). If we were good Christians, we might say that at one time in his life, Jesus had a more modest opinion of himself, but, later on, he came to understand himself as the incarnation of God. Trying to be objective about the text, which seems to contradict itself in some places, we might say that Jesus may have thought one thing about himself, but his disciples saw something else about him. For example, Buddha is worshipped as God in the Far East, but Buddha himself did not even believe in God! Once a great man dies, what he becomes through the evolution of fact and legend can be something entirely different from what he was. Nonetheless, for our purposes, we have to assume that all of the events and statements in the New Testament have equal weight. Such being the case, we would have to conclude that Jesus was not a prophet in the classical Jewish sense. To be sure, Jesus quotes the Prophets constantly. He was fond of quoting Hosea's teaching: "I, the Lord, desire mercy (*hesed*) and not formal ceremony."[12] He quotes from the Book of Leviticus, "Thou shalt love thy neighbor as thyself" (Lev 19:18), and he quoted Rabbi Hillel's Golden Rule, "Do unto others as you would have them do unto you."[13] The Jesus described in the New Testament was more than a teacher of the ethical Jewish tradition. Two names were applied to him; one was Messiah (or Christ) and the other was the "Son of Man" or "Son of God." To discuss Jesus, we have to understand these terms.

---

12. "formal ceremony" or "sacrifices" (Hosea 6:6).
13. Hillel, who lived 50 years earlier, said it this way, "Do not do unto others what you would not have them do unto you." See also Leviticus 19, "Love thy neighbor, etc."

Was He the Messiah?

The traditional Jewish view of the Messiah, as defined by the Prophets, is that a flesh and blood son will be born to a descendent of King David who will rule over an independent Israel, who will overthrow the foreign power, and usher in an era of peace and justice. The word Messiah means "anointed one," but the text of the New Testament tells us that Jesus did not like the phrase, "The descendent (or son) of David." He preferred the phrase "the Son of Man" or "the Son of God" (Matt 22:41-46). It is important for all students of this period to try to understand these latter phrases. The doctrine of "Son of Man" refers to a time when a semi-divine being (a Son of God) will come in the clouds, judge the nations, separate the good people from evil people, assign the good to high reward, and assign the evil to Hell.[14] The earlier Prophets of Israel knew nothing of this doctrine of "The Son of Man." Certainly, it was not involved in their teachings. This doctrine belongs to a later period, since the bulk of the great prophets were from five to eight hundred years earlier than Jesus. (The Prophet Ezekiel uses the term "Son of man" (ch. 2:1-3) to mean merely himself, i.e., a human being). Jesus may have interpreted the phrase just as Ezekiel did.

The learned and intellectual Jews completely rejected the doctrine of the "Son of God," for, to them, it smacked of paganism. The Jews knew of one God who related directly to His children. The pagan religions all spoke of their king

---

14. See the discussion, "Judaism", Vol. 2, G.F. Moore, Harvard University Press, 1950, pp. 330-340; Moore traces the development of the simple messianic doctrine into later fusions. The more fanciful notions of Esdras and Baruch were not considered worthy of inclusion in the Jewish Bible (Tanach). C.f. F.C. Grant, *Ancient Judaism & The New Testament*, pp. 70ff on "The Son of Man." See also Grant, pp 132-133.

as being the chief son of God. In the New Testament, we hear much talk of hell and fire and brimstone. Satan is a prominent figure there, whereas our "Literary Prophets" did not believe in a separate deity who was the Lord of Evil. The New Testament speaks of demons, little devils, who got into people and made them insane or infirm. We know from the Talmud that some of the Rabbis of this period also spoke of demons. Jesus is presented as an exorcisor of those demons. In the Middle Ages, orthodox Jews had a procedure to exorcise a demon (a *dybuk*). The Catholic Church has retained such a procedure.

Our Prophets never spoke of demons. They didn't believe in them, even as most modern people do not believe in demons. Much of the fame of Jesus, according to the New Testament, is based on his ability to chase away demons and to heal the sick. Earlier, we spoke about two Hebrew prophets, Elijah and Elisha, who, we are told, healed the sick.[15] We tried to show how many of the same stories about Elijah and Elisha are told about Jesus in the New Testament, with some extensions. Still, when our Hebrew Bible tells us that Elijah brought a young man back to life or cured a leper, we don't attribute deity to him, nor do we necessarily consider these healing prophets among our greater prophets. For us, the essence of religion is not miraculous healing of this type, but a courageous insistence on the uplifting of our fellow human beings. The prophet Elisha, even when he was himself dead, caused another man to be resurrected from the dead; yet, usually we count Elisha as among our lesser prophets.[16] Not even resurrection is sufficient for us to deify a man born of woman.

---

15. See "Similarities between Jesus and Elijah – Elisha," our Chapter 2.
16. See our Chapter 2.

Challenge to the Priests

These are some interesting comparisons between the life of Jeremiah and Jesus, although Jeremiah antedated Jesus by, at least, 600 years. Let us compare the Temple scene in which Jesus is described as overturning the tables of the money changers and the Temple scene involving Jeremiah, many hundreds of years earlier. Jesus, we are told, came into the Temple, which in his time was run by the Sadducees, or Jews who were Roman quislings,[17] and he declared, "It is written, "My house shall be called a house of prayer, but you make it a den of robbers'" (Matt 21:12-13). We note that Jesus did not make a declaration in the name of God as a prophet does. He merely quoted from Jewish scripture. Now let us turn back the years and come to Jeremiah

In his time, the Temple was controlled by a powerful and highly entrenched Jewish priesthood that had seldom been challenged. To the large number of people assembled in the Temple for prayer, Jeremiah said, in the name of God, "Will you steal, murder, commit adultery, swear falsely, and burn incense to Baal… and, then, come and stand before Me in this House and say, 'We are delivered.' Has this house, which is called by My name, become a den of robbers in your eyes?" (Jer. 7:9ff). Please note that Jesus, 600 years later, uses the exact phrase "A den of robbers."[18] In the New Testament we are told that Jesus overturns the tables of those selling pigeons to the people. These pigeons were used for sacrifices in the Temple.

---

17. Quisling was famous as a collaborator with the Nazis. Therefore, a "quisling" is a collaborator. The role of the High Priest in those days was a political appointment. The Pharisees were less friendly with the Romans and less assimilated to the culture of the conquering nation.
18. Jesus knows he is quoting Jeremiah.

Jeremiah, told the priests, the people being present, God does not wish these sacrifices, nor did He ever command them (Jer. 7:21). It seems clear that the story concerning Jesus in the Temple is patterned, after the dramatic, and more detailed, Jeremiah story.

The Trials

There are also strong resemblances (and differences) between the trial of Jeremiah and the trial of Jesus. Jeremiah had been accused of treason for urging the people not to fight against the Babylonians, who were attacking the city of Jerusalem. Further, he had criticized the Judean king and the nobles for not having the interests of the poor at heart. Jeremiah had been placed in the public stocks, and some had spat on him as they walked by. Jeremiah had identified with the needs of the poor, but he had made no pretense to be a healer, as Elijah had been 250 years earlier, nor did he pretend to work "miracles." The formula of Jeremiah was simple; justice would bring peace and prosperity; injustice would bring war and famine. The account of his trial, which is found in detail in the 26th chapter of the book which bears the Prophet's name, tells us that the priests and the professional prophets (i.e., those who were in the king's pay) brought him to trial and asked for his death. The princes and the people, however, in the second trial, asked for his release. The reason they presented for acquittal was simple, "Our tradition is that a man speaking his conscience may not be punished."[19] Jeremiah was released (see 26:16ff).

The trial involving Jesus, however, was under vastly different circumstances. In the first place, the final court was a Roman court. Only the Roman Governor could judge his guilt or innocence. We are told that there was first a religious

19. This is a paraphrase of the statements in Jeremiah 26:16ff.

trial, during which the High Priest, a Roman appointee, asked Jesus the question, "Are you the Messiah, the Son of God?" (Matt 26:63). We have said before that the High Priest, although Jewish, was a Roman quisling. Still, his question is hardly a Jewish question. The question implies that the Messiah and the Son of God are one and the same. We have already discussed that, for Jews, the Messiah was merely a human descendent of King David,[20] while the "Son of God" was something else again. Jesus seems to answer that he is associated with the "Son of Man," The council adjudges him worthy of death, and he is taken to the Roman Judicial court. Compare Jeremiah 26:7-8 where, "The priests and the prophets (i.e., prophets paid by the ruling power) and all the people initially pronounced a verdict of guilty."[21]

The Roman governor, Pontius Pilate, has an entirely different question for Jesus. He is not concerned with the religious aspects of Messiah or the phrase Son of God, since he doesn't accept those nuances anyhow. Pilate asks a straight forward political question, "Are you the King of the Jews?" (Matt 27:11). Pilate understood correctly that if Jesus were, indeed, the Messiah, the political consequences of that title was that the people would follow him in his attempt to overthrow the Roman government and to usher in an independent Jewish state. In that role, Jesus was a real threat to the Romans who were already having difficulty controlling these stiff-necked Jews.

The New Testament text, then, takes a peculiar twist. It tells us that Pilate, who had unceremoniously crucified thousands of Jews, decided that he did not really want to punish this one, but he yielded to the cries of the "multitude" to kill him. Why they wanted him killed when they would benefit the most, if he were

---

20. Could Jesus have been saying, "I am just a human being?" See also Ezekiel's use of the phrase.
21. This was, apparently, the ecclesiastical trial to be followed by a secular trial.

the Messiah or King of Judea, is something the New Testament does not explain. The authors of this story apparently did not understand that the interests of the people were not with the priests any more than that the interests of the Pharisees were with the priests (the latter being dependent on Roman largesse).

The Book of Jeremiah tells us that the Prophet influenced the people enough so that they gave little resistance to the Babylonians attacking them, yet Jeremiah was not killed for his obvious treason. Jesus seemed to be much less of a threat, yet he was killed. The difference is, at least in part, the difference between the mercy of a Jewish court and the practice of a foreign or Roman court.

We can conclude that while Jesus was in some ways after the manner of a prophet, his association with terms like Messiah gave him a political aspect not shared by prophets before him; and his connection with the term "Son of God" gives him an association that takes him well beyond the boundaries of Judaism. Still, in all fairness, it must be said, that most of the teachings of Jesus were within the Jewish tradition, and that, as a weaver of parables, he was a master. Jews can learn something about Judaism by reading the New Testament and profit from it.

Who Was Released?

One final speculation. The New Testament says that Pontius Pilate offered to release one of two prisoners found guilty that day. One prisoner was called, "Jesus, the Christ" (Matt 27:17ff); the other was called "Barabbas" (Matt 27:16ff). The text indicates that the "people" asked Pilate to crucify "Jesus the Christ" and to release Barabbas. The interesting point is that Barabbas is an Aramaic name meaning, "The Son of the Father." The name raises the question, who was crucified, after all, if "The Son of the Father" was released? Add to this the fact that some New Testament scholars hold that some ancient texts do not merely say "Barabbas," but *Jesus* Barabbas.[22]

Suppose that we should read Matthew 27:21, as some ancient texts apparently read, in this fashion. "Which of the two do you want me to release for you?! And they said, *"Jesus* Barabbas." This would then present us with this possibility: Jesus, the Christ (Messiah) was crucified, but Jesus, the Son of the Father, was not. This opens up the whole question as to whether there were not two distinct personalities adding up to the one Jesus described in the New Testament. If we read back to the separate religious and political trials described in Matthew, we will recall that the Priests had condemned the man who called himself the "Son of God," whereas the Romans were most concerned about the man who called himself, "King of the Jews," that is, the Messiah. If there were indeed two men, bearing the name Jesus, then it is possible that the man condemned by the priestly court, was later released by the wish of the masses.[23] This would place the responsibility for such crucifixion as took place squarely where it belongs, on the Roman plunderers of Judea.[24]

It is interesting to note that in an ancient Persian book we have this statement – Zoroaster, the Persian prophet – was killed by the priest of the older religion. Zoraster lived around 500 B.C.E.

---

22. *The Holy Bible: The Revised Standard Version*, (T. Nelson and Sons, N.Y., 1953) says in a note, pg. 36, "Other ancient authorities read *Jesus* Barabbas."
23. Note that although Jeremiah was condemned to death by the priests; after the secular trial, the people and the Princes) voted for his release. The pattern could be similar here.
24. For a detailed discussion of the background of the trials, see S. Zeitlin, *Who Crucified Jesus?*, especially Chapter X. He points out, "Neither Peter nor Paul accused the Jews of crucifying Jesus," pg. 177. And again, "The Apostolic Fathers never accused the Jews of the crucifixion of Jesus," pg. 179. All of these, according to Zeitlin, merely understood that the priests had turned Jesus over to Pilate who condemned and sentenced him. So, the Roman historian Tacitus (*Annals* 15:44).

Chapter 3

The Book of Isaiah

Some Christian scholars hold that Isaiah (the second Isaiah) prophesizes the coming of Jesus along with his suffering of cosmic proportions. The Christian belief is that because of the suffering of Jesus (i.e., The Crucifixion), all those who believe in him will be forgiven for their sins as vicarious beneficiaries.

Jews, on the other hand, long before the birth of Jesus, interpreted Isaiah, in an entirely different fashion. After all, Isaiah was a prophet in Israel, and his proclamations have long been part of the Hebrew Scriptures. Certainly,[25] Jews have the right to interpret their own Scriptures, and it seems rather odd to them that they are told that their interpretation is wrong by someone outside the Israelite experience.

To the Jews, it has been clear from their own writing and experience that when the Hebrew Scripture refers to "God's

---

25. All scripture quotations in this chapter are from "The Prophets (*Nevi'im*)" in a new translation of "The Holy Scriptures according to the Masoretic Text," The Jewish Publication Society of America, Philadelphia 1978.

Servant," it is talking about the Israelite people as a unit.

In the first section of the Book of Isaiah (previous to Chapter 53), there is constant reference to Israel as the Servant of God who is suffering *in the present*. In Chapter 51, it is Jerusalem which has "drunk the cup of His Wrath."

In Chapter 52, the Prophet speaks of Jerusalem again, which has suffered as a punishment for its failure to obey God's will. Now, however, we read in the text, God will "loose the bonds from your neck, O captive one, Fair Zion." Now, however, declares the Prophet, God will redeem His people. "Just as the many were appalled at him. So marred was his appearance, unlike that of man. His form beyond human semblance" (v. 14) and now –My servant shall prosper" (v. 13).

The theme continues almost unbroken in Ch. 53, v. 3, "He was despised, shunned by men…(v. 4) "yet it was our sickness that he was bearing. Our suffering that he endured…(v. 5) but he was wounded because of our sins, crushed because of our impurities. He bore the chastisement that made us whole. And by his bruises we were healed"….v. 11, "My righteous servant made the many righteous…." The Prophet made it clear that he is speaking of the suffering of Israel in exile and God is now promising a return of the exiles and an end to their suffering. (Ch. 54:1ff): "For a while I forsook you, but with vast love I will bring you back" (v. 7).

V. 8 "…But with kindness everlasting I will take you back in love."
V. 17 "… 'Such is the lot of the servants of the Lord'… declares the Lord."

In Verse 17 of Ch. 54, in the Book of Isaiah we see the use of the word "servant" (singular). This would seem to support the view of those scholars who claim that God is speaking of His entire people as His servants. Likewise, the term "Jerusalem" is used to mean the same as the people. Therefore, we have the expression, ch. 52:9b ... "for the Lord will comfort His people, will redeem Jerusalem."

In spite of the seeming clarity here, there seems to be an added dimension when the Prophet Isaiah uses expressions associated to the Temple worship procedures. In 53:10 we have the expression "offering of guilt." Some scholars see this phrase as to a prophet who was unjustly persecuted, perhaps Jeremiah, perhaps even Isaiah himself (see Blenkinsopp).[26]

However difficult it may be to translate words written hundreds of years ago, it seems clear that Isaiah is mediating God's intent to cause a major reversal in the fortunes of Israel/Judah and to bring about the change in the immediate future. It seems clear that the suffering servants suffered in the past (and are not to suffer some hundreds of years later).

On the other hand, we cannot disavow the fact that a group of Jews and Gentiles, later to begin a new religion, chose to put a different interpretation on those biblical words. We should try to understand the events in Jewish history which led to this later development. The limited purposes of our book restrain us from delving into all of these factors.

---

26. *A History of Prophecy in Israel*, Joseph Blenkinsopp.

Chapter 4

The "Individual" Who Suffers in Isaiah 53

The general scholarly opinion is that the "individual" described as suffering in Isaiah 53 is not an individual at all, but he is a personification for the entire people of Israel.

There is a statement however, in some Jewish sources that the victim is none other than Isaiah himself. In the pseudepigraphic *Ascension of Isaiah*, the author observes that Isaiah was sown asunder by the wicked King Manasseh (517ff); cf. Heb. 11:37.

In the Babylonian Talmud (*yer.* 496) also Jerusalem Talmud (T) *snh*10:2, 28c, we are told that Isaiah hid in a cedar tree which was "sawn asunder." All of these sources agree that the Prophet was martyred in the reign of King Manasseh.

While this assumption is a possibility, it has not been seriously accepted by most scholars. The evidence seems overwhelming that the sufferer is the people Israel itself.

Chapter 5

The Book of Daniel

Most biblical scholars tend to think the Book of Daniel is one of the later books of the Hebrew Scriptures. Nonetheless, it contains a description of concepts in which many Jews came to believe.

The Book is dominated by a description of miraculous events in the life of Daniel and his close friends. Set in the time after the Babylonians conquest of Judea, it tells of Daniel's service to the Babylonian King as an interpreter of dreams. In this service, Daniel pleases the King more than do the native Babylonian advisors (i.e., the magicians and enchanters).

In his interpretation of the King's dreams, Daniel introduces the King to the Judean "God of heaven," who alone reveals secrets involving future events. Naturally, the native Babylonian advisors are jealous of the favor this foreigner, Daniel, has obtained in the King's eyes. They hatch a plot to catch Daniel disobeying a royal decree which conflicts with Daniel's religion. Daniel has to be punished, and he is cast into a fiery furnace along with his equally guilty friends. We are told that Daniel's God saves them from the fire, and they are spared from further punishment by the king.

Nebuchadnezzar, the King, had a second dream which Daniel alone interpreted for him. He advised the King that in spite of his might and riches, the "God in heaven," Daniel's God would punish him for his false pride and misuse of his power. He advised the King to change his ways, to help the poor and to confess his sins. The King could not overcome his pride and arrogance, so he was punished by the loss of his vast kingdom.

After some time, Nebuchadnezzar, now a humble man bereft of his power and riches, repented and worshipped "the Most High" the God of Daniel, who determined events in the world. The King was restored to his kingdom and power.

Daniel, himself, had some elaborate visions concerning "the end of days," which fortell the return of the captive Judeans to their homeland. In his vision, he is addressed by a heaven-sent messenger as "son of man," a term also used by the Prophet Ezekiel and Daniel.[27] The phrase "son of man" means only a human being and who, in this case, one who receives a divine message. It is possible that Jesus understands the term in just the same sense.

In speaking of the deliverance of the Judeans, the narrative in The Book of Daniel reads: (ch. 12:2ff) "and many of them that sleep in the dust of the earth shall awake, some to everlasting life, and some to… everlasting abhorrence.…"[28]

---

27. Dan. 8:16-17.
28. Dan. 12:2 (The Holy Scriptures according to the Masoretic Text, A New

The Book of Daniel is important to us because it demonstrates that the Jews of this later time believed in the resurrection of the righteous dead. Many of the Pharisees believed in this doctrine, as apparently did Jesus and his followers. It is a doctrine not found in the books of the Hebrew Scriptures compiled earlier than the Book of Daniel, but it is clearly stated here.

In Judaism, God is the Judge who administers the ultimate judgment, but in Christianity that role falls to Jesus as the Son of God. In medieval Europe, many Christians grew fearful of Jesus as the stern judge and looked to Mary as the compassionate one. In this period, many churches dedicated to Mary were built.

Translation, The Jewish Publication Society of America, Philadelphia, 1955).

Chapter 6

The Jewishness of Jesus

Julius Wellhausen, the famous Biblical scholar, once proclaimed "Jesus was not a Christian, he was a Jew."[29] His allegiance was to the will of God as spelled out in the Torah (the first Five Books of Moses) and, in the other Jewish literature extant in his time.

When asked by a scribe, "which is the first of all the Commandments?" Jesus quoted from Jewish scripture alone, i.e., "Thou shalt love the Lord thy God with all thy might, etc." and "Thou shalt love thy neighbor as thyself."[30]

When Jesus instructed his disciples to go out and teach his message, he restricted their area of teaching to the "Lost sheep of Israel." [31]

---

29. Quoted by the highly respected historian Dr. Joseph Klausner in his "Jesus of Nazareth," p. 363 (published by the Macmillan Company, New York, 1925).
30. The first part is from the Book of Deuteronomy, (6:5) and the second is from the Book of Leviticus, (19:18) both in The Torah, cf. Mark 12:28-32.
31. Matthew 10:5-6.

It was not until the time of Paul that the religion Paul defined was to be aimed at all the peoples. Paul is the real founder of Christianity, not Jesus, and Paul, who never saw Jesus, was so influenced by Hellenism himself, that he brought a strong influence of Greek philosophy into the Jewish Teaching of Jesus. The blend is known as Christianity.[32]

---

[32]. At the very end of Matthew (28:19) we are told that after his resurrection, Jesus seems to broaden this commission, i.e., he wants his message taken to all the people, not just the Jews.

Chapter 7

The Pharisees

In the New Testament, Jesus is quoted on several occasions as being highly critical of the Pharisees. The Pharisees were one of three major sects or parties in the Jewish community at the time Jesus lived. Because of the phrasing of these criticisms, many readers of the New Testament assume that of all the sects in the Jewish community, Jesus was most opposed in the Pharisees. There is considerable evidence to the contrary.

One of the three major sects was the Sadducees or the priesthood and their followers. Most of the latter were highly conservative and wealthy people. They did not accept the oral law as developed by the scribes (scholars) and strictly observed by the Pharisees, many of whom were outstanding scholars themselves. The Pharisees, then, were interested in expanding the laws in the Pentateuch (the Torah), the first five books of the Hebrew Scripture, to meet the changing social conditions. The laws the Scribes and Pharisees developed were called the Oral Law, in the sense that they were not written in the Pentateuch. To the Pharisees, the Oral Law had equal authority to the so-called written law. The Sadducees, the conservative sect, both religiously and politically, were seen as enemies of a developing Judaism. On the other hand, the Pharisees were open to the guidance of the Hebrew Prophets but strictly observant of the newer rituals in the Oral Law. The Sadducees substantially ignored the oral laws and ritual which were so important to the Pharisees.

The priesthood under Roman rule consisted of appointees of the Romans. Their alliances with the Romans did not obtain popular approval, while the Pharisees neutrality to political maneuvering attracted the middle class and many of the poorer people. The teaching of Jesus, "Render unto Caesar the things that are Caesar's and unto God the things that are God's," is Pharisaic teaching. Indeed, many of the teachings of Jesus indicated that he was himself a Pharisee.

Since there were some Pharisees who criticized others among themselves for making too much of a public display of their religion, Jesus could simply have been among these fault finders but hardly completely against all of his teachers and comrades.

"The Pharisees believed in the survival of the soul, the revival of the body, the great judgment, and the life of the world to come."[33] The Sadducees did not, because the Hebrew Scripture said nothing of these matters, except for the late Book of Daniel.

---

33 G.F. Moore, *Judaism*, Vol. I, p. 6

Chapter 8

Understanding Jesus

The New Testament presents Jesus as a Jewish teacher immersed in his traditional background but belonging to the apocryphal group. The latter means he is anticipating a revolutionary change in the nature of the social world with God as the victor over the opponents of His people, and the poor and suffering emerging as triumphant over their oppressors.

A second type of the characterization of Jesus is presented from the Pauline theological view.[34] That is, Jesus is the divine Christ who died for the remission of the sins of all, who was resurrected, and in whom we all live. Paul believed that if we share the faith in him, his spirit will live in us. This latter characterization influenced by Paul's Hellenistic orientation,[35] rejects the importance of the Mosaic Law (although Jesus affirms that law) and Paul places faith, rather than deeds, in

---

34 Paul, a Jew, is the author of several books included in The New Testament Canon. He never saw Jesus, and he is not the author of any of the synoptic Gospels.
35 See Corinthians 51:14-21.

the center of religiosity. Paul claimed to be "blameless" in his observance of pharisaic Judaism, but he did not require the observance of pharisaic ceremonies from his converts.

Today most Christians emphasize the crucified Christ who bore the sins of others and was resurrected, promising eternal life to his believers. Many, not all, of the Jewish ceremonies Jesus and Paul observed as Jews are not followed by modern Christians.

Chapter 9

The "Son of God"

In the Hebrew Scriptures, we are told that all people (male and female) are created in the "image of God" (Genesis 1:27). In this proclamation, there is no distinction made between people of various nations, races, or social standing.

The Prophet Amos makes it clear that chosenness means no more than the granting of special responsibility. The Prophet declares that God has also redeemed the Philistines and the Syrians among others (9:7).

Philo, the great Jewish philosopher of the Hellenistic period, states, "All who have real knowledge of the Creator and Father of All Things are rightly called "Sons of God." ("On the Confusion of Language")

The Gospel speaks of one divine son, apart from the other humans (Matthew 11:27, Mark 10:45). In the New Testament, Jesus states, "No one knoweth the Father, save the Son and he to whomsoever the Son willeth to reveal him" (Matthew 11:27). This idea of the relationship of people to God asserts that there must be a mediator between God and His children, and Jesus is that sole and required mediator.

Jews see this teaching as opposed in the idea that all humans are created in "the image of God," and therefore, all stand equal before Him.

In the book of Jeremiah, the Prophet quoted God as saying, "Joseph (Israel) has ever been my son." Elsewhere the Prophet presents the same idea when he substitutes the name Ephrayim for Joseph. Ephrayim[36] was the son of Joseph. Both of these names are symbolic for the people Israel.

---

36 Ephrayim is spelled with or without the "y," i.e., Ephraim.

Chapter 10

The Crucifixion

A central part of the Christian faith today is the crucifixion of Jesus by the Romans. Even in the description of the prayers of Jesus, as he was thus suffering, we are told that he uttered a well-known Jewish Psalm (Psalm 22). How are we told this? In Mark 15:34, we are told that Jesus uttered Psalm 22. The text of the apostle specifies that Jesus prayed the first line of the Psalm in Aramaic, the colloquial language spoken by Jews, "My God, My God why have you forsaken me?" (See also Matthew 27:46, where Hebrew was used.)

It was a wide spread practice among the Jews of that time to indicate the entire Psalm by reciting the first line only. It is as if the first line was regarded as the name or title of the Psalm.[37] In the 22nd Psalm, there is also reference to the casting of lots by one's afflicters in order to strip the victim of his garments. The apostles tell us that the Roman soldiers did exactly this, casting lots to strip Jesus of his clothing (in this case, royal clothing), see Matthew 27:35. Here again we see the attempt in the New Testament to fulfill an event

---

[37] A common practice, the implication is that Jesus prayed the entire Psalm 22.

found in the Hebrew Scriptures, in this case, in the Psalms.

Could it be that the purpose of the repetitions and references are to prove to Jewish observers that Jesus fulfilled all that is indicated about a coming Messiah? This would indicate that the early leaders, of what became a new religion, were Jews speaking to other Jews.

Some scholars believe that the two men crucified along with Jesus were brigands or revolutionaries. If this is so, it adds evidence to the view that the Romans crucified Jesus, because they believed that he was also a revolutionary.

While the crucifixion is a central part of most Christian belief today, some of the apostles do not speak much of it. Some of the early church fathers do not speak of the crucifixion.

Paul, who never saw Jesus, nevertheless makes the crucifixion a significant part of his teaching, and through him the act becomes central to other teachers and to some authors of the New Testament Books.

In considering the New Testament account of the crucifixion, we should note the account of the death of the Iranian prophet, Zoroaster, in the lost book of the Avesta.

The historian George Foote Moore tells us that Zoroaster,[38] who was said to have a miraculous birth (600 B.C.), was murdered at his age of 77. He was killed, as the account goes, by a priest of the old religion.

---

38 P. 363. *History of Religions*, vol. 1, Charles Scribner & Sons, NY, 1946, Revised edition. Zoroaster lived about 500 years before Jesus.

Chapter 11

Which Messiah?

In the Tanakh (The Hebrew Bible), which some call the Old Testament, we are informed that those appointed by God to lead His people are officially anointed with holy oil by the reigning prophet (God's representative). The person thus anointed is the "anointed one" or Mashiach, in Hebrew. Among God's chosen leaders are the high priests and the kings. Technically each person so anointed is a messiah.

Even a person outside of the Israelite community can be chosen by God to lead Israel. Thus, in the Book of Isaiah (Chap. 45:1), we are told that Cyrus, King of Persia, is chosen to lead to freedom those Israelites living in captivity in Babylonia and Assyria. Cyrus is named by God, Isaiah tells us, to be "His anointed one," His messiah.

The meaning of the Hebrew word for messiah changed as the centuries passed. After Babylonia conquered Judea (the Southern part of the divided Israelite kingdom) and took captive a significant part of the Judean leadership, the Prophets began to speak of an ideal King who would be installed as King (Messiah) when the Judean nation regained its freedom and the former captives, or their decedents, were restored to their own land.

The Prophet Jeremiah proclaims in the name of God, "See, a time is coming when I will raise up a true branch of David's line. He shall reign as King and shall prosper, and he shall do what is just and right in the land... and this is the name by which he shall be called, 'the Lord is our vindicator.'"

The Second Isaiah (Chap. 40ff) is sometimes identified as the Prophet of The Exile. Isaiah clearly speaks of Israel, the people, as God's chosen servant which had become "...the despised being, the abhorred nation" which was persecuted and mistreated by it's conquerors (Chap. 49:7, Chap. 53:7-11).

At first, the Prophets justify the military conquest of both northern and southern Kingdoms by alien nations by proclaiming that the God of Israel had permitted this to happen, because the Israelites had not followed God's law. The Israelite religious leaders could not believe that foreign military powers could conquer the Israelite nations, if the latter had deserved God's favor. They concluded that the God of the Israelite nations was more powerful than all other gods. They believed that international events were under the control of the Israelite God, and other nations were merely the tools or pawns of the Israelite God.[39]

When the conquering nations (Babylonia and Assyria) seemed to be overly cruel to God's chosen people, God pardoned His people for their waywardness and punished the former conquerors. The Prophet Jeremiah explicitly proclaimed (in God's name) "...I am ever a father to Israel. Ephraim is my firstborn" (Chap. 31:9).

Jeremiah proclaims in God's name, "'See, a time is coming' – declares the Lord – 'when I will make a new covenant with the House of Israel and the House of Judah. It will not be like

---

39 Matthew 1:1-16 and Luke 3:23-38.

the covenant I made with their fathers, when I took them by the hand to lead them out of the land of Egypt, but a covenant which they broke, so that I rejected them' – declares the Lord. 'But such is the covenant I will make with the House of Israel after these days' – declares the Lord: 'I will put My teaching into their inmost being and inscribe it upon their hearts. Then I will be their God, and they shall be My people. No longer will they need to teach one another and say to one another, Heed the Lord; for all of them, from the least of them to the greatest, shall heed Me', declares the Lord; 'For I will forgive their iniquities, and remember their sins no more.'" (Chap. 31:31-34)[40]

The authors of the New Testament go to some length to establish a strong link between Jesus and King David. No doubt this is to demonstrate that Jesus is the ideal future king of whom several of the Literary Prophets speak. Thus, he is claimed to be not only a King (Mashiach, anointed one) but also *the* Messiah, the ideal King who will overthrow the foreign power, (Rome, in the current situation) and establish the reign of righteousness. The Romans understood Jesus to be just such a claimant to the throne of an independent Judea, for they wrote on his cross, we are told, the four Roman letters INRI. Each of these letters stood for a Roman word: (I= Jesus, N= Nazareth, R= Rex-King, I = Judea). The Roman soldiers further mocked Jesus by giving him a purple robe. Purple is the royal color, and the soldiers gave him a crown (of thorns). All of these factors indicate that the Romans thought of Jesus as a revolutionary.

Jesus, however, may have thought of himself not as the Messiah ben David (a descendent of David) but as someone else.

Some scholars think Jesus and his followers thought of himself as Messiah ben Joseph, sometimes identified

---

[40] Jeremiah here emphasizes the New Covenant is between Judah and Israel and involves no other people. This translation is from "The Holy Scriptures, A New Translation."

as Messiah ben Ephraim. Ephraim was the son of Joseph. The belief that there were two messiahs was held by certain groups in Judaism as evidenced in the literature known as "The Dead Sea Scrolls." The Jewish authors of these scrolls indicate that their group believed in two messiahs, each of whom had a specific function. Certain of the apocryphal books[41] also refer to the Messiah ben Joseph. This messiah was to come before the Messiah ben David, and he was to suffer a tragic death in battle.

We first learn of the tradition of the Messiah ben Joseph in the Babylonian Talmud (Sukkah 52a). In a seventh-century apocalyptic text know as Sefer Zerubabel, we are told that Messiah ben Joseph was killed by the wicked Armilus but was resurrected by the Messiah ben David and the Prophet Elijah. This reference seems to be a post Christian development, but we have a pre-Christian reference to the Messiah ben Joseph in the Dead Sea Scrolls and in the newly discovered stone text which is similar to the Dead Sea writings. This stone is identified as "Gabriel's Revelation" and seems to speak of the Messiah ben Joseph.[42]

In the Apocryphal work "Joseph and Aseneth"[43] written between 100 BCE and 115 CE, Joseph is described as "son of God" (6:35, 18:13) Joseph is also called "God's firstborn son" (18:11, 21:4, 23:10). Also, see Jeremiah 31:19.

In "The Testament of the Twelve Patriarchs,"[44] from the second Temple period, the Testament of Benjamin connects Joseph and the figure of the suffering servant (Chap. 52-83). This seems to demonstrate that there are sources from the Second Temple period that are already referring to Joseph

---

[41] The books not accepted in the official canon of the Hebrew Bible. Many of these books are preserved in the Catholic Bible or elsewhere.
[42] See the article, "The Messiah Son of Joseph," pp. 58ff in *Biblical Archaeology Review*, September/October 2008, Vol. 3 and number 5.
[43] ibid.
[44] ibid.

as having a special relationship to the developing messianic thought.

In the Midrash "Pesikta Rabati,"[45] there is a reference to a Messiah Ephraim (son of Joseph) who is asked to take upon himself the suffering of all of Israel. There is apparently a scholarly difference of opinion as to whether these writings precede or follow the New Testament.

On the other hand, Jesus is called the "Son of David" many times in the New Testament (Mark 10:47-48, 11:10, Matthew 9:27, 12:23, 15:22, 20:30-31. 21-9, Luke 18:38-39). The Nativity Story (Matthew 2:1-18, Luke 2:1-20) seems designed to make clear that Jesus is the "Son of David" and therefore, the Messiah.

In his seminal book, *The Messiah Idea In Jewish History*,[46] Julius H. Greenstone shows that there is the concept of two messiahs, Messiah ben Joseph (who leads Israel in battles against its enemies and is himself killed), and Messiah ben David, who is to conquer the foreign overlord and lead Israel to freedom and righteousness.

In the light of evidence, both in the New Testament and in extra-testamentary information, we have to conclude that in the matter of the messiah, we do not have clarity. The New Testament may not conclude that Jesus is the triumphant Messiah, son of David.

In any event, the Jewish understanding of the latter as described by the Literary Prophets requires a number of factors not fulfilled by Jesus. These are: (1) the ideal King was to overthrow the foreign power (Rome). This did not happen. (2) A long period of peace was to be introduced. (3) The ideal King would rule in justice. (4) The two divided nations, Israel to the north and Judea to the south, will be united, and the

---

45 ibid.
46 Published 1906 and reprinted in 1943 by the Jewish Publication Society of America.

suffering of the combined nations would cease. Few, if any, of these provisions occurred.

If the New Testament does not make clear which Messiah Jesus and his followers think he is, the Romans are clear in their thinking that Jesus is a claimant to the throne of an independent Judea. The High Priest, as described in the New Testament, agrees with the Romans. If the people were given a voice in the situation, it would be extremely odd if they would not hope that Jesus was, indeed the Messiah ben David, for that would mean the overthrowing of the cruel Roman master!

Down through the centuries to come, the people were attracted to every claimant to be the Messiah ben David. Each pretender would attract a huge following, sometimes to the great hurt of the people.[47] There is no reason to believe that the people would not follow Jesus also, but those in power, i.e., the Romans and their appointee, the High Priest, would have another reason to be alarmed.

At another point in the New Testament, the text suggests that Jesus thought of himself as the disciple of John the Baptist or as something more than that. We are told that Jesus was baptized by John and sometime later engaged in a discussion with his own disciples as to whom they thought he (Jesus) was. They said, "some say John the Baptist, some Elijah, and others Jeremiah, or one of the prophets."[48]

The text then tells us that Jesus tries to get a more specific answer. He says, "But who say you that I am?" Simon Peter answered and said, "thou art the Christ, the son of the living God." The story continues, "And Jesus blessed him… and promised to deliver unto him, the keys of the kingdom of Heaven." Then Jesus charges his disciples to tell no man that he was the Christ.

---

[47] See *The Messiah Idea in History*, Julius Greenstone, especially page 110.

A few days later, the disciples suggested that the Scribes taught that Elijah is expected to come first. To this, Jesus replied that Elijah had already appeared, "and they knew him not…." "Then the disciples understood that he was speaking to them of John the Baptist."

All of this seems simple and clear. Jesus is making the case that he fulfills all the requirements for the Messiah as expressed in the Talmud and as generally understood by the Jewish authorities.[49]

In this passage, he believes that he is not the Messiah ben David, but someone higher than that…. This someone is identified in Psalm 110, v. 1 as "Lord,"[50] according to the New Testament interpretation. Jewish scholars read their native text differently.

Psalm 110, like the other Psalms, is attributed to King David. Many of the Psalms are of a general nature and may be recited as a personal prayer by anyone. See, for example, the widely used 23rd Psalm ("The Lord is my Shepherd…"). On the other hand, many of the Psalms seem to be rendered by a king concerned about problems attending to his reign. The 23rd Psalm can also be rendered in this mood. In this author's doctoral thesis, he analyzes the 23rd Psalm from just this viewpoint.[51]

In the Tanach, The Holy Scriptures,[52] Psalm 110 seems clearly to be written for David but not by David. David is called "my lord," but the latter word is distinguished from the word "Lord," which is reserved for God. David and his rule

---

[49] See Greenstone, *Messiah Idea…*, pp. 187-88 where Maimonides place the requirements for the Messiah under 10 points.
[50] For that would bring on danger.
[51] "The Meaning of the Hebrew Word "Tov" in the Scripture," found in the Library of The Hebrew Union College – Jewish Institute of Religion, New York, NY.
[52] Published by the Jewish Publication Society, Philadelphia, PA, 1985.

are favored by God, and the Psalm asserts that David and his descendants will rule forever. "You are a priest forever, a rightful King in my decree" (v. 4b).

The Hebrew script uses different words to describe God and David. God is יהוה the singular word for the name of the Hebrew God. Since the name of יהוה is not to be spoken except by the High Priest on the holiest of days, it was given the vowels of the word for "master," so that it might be used in common speech.[53] The four letter word for the Hebrew name of God was then expressed in English by some as "Jehovah." In Hebrew the name of God sounds like "master" (Ah-do-nai), but this is not God's specific name which grammatically is related to the verb "To be."

At any rate, there are two different Hebrew words in Psalm 110:1. A proper reading might be יהוה said to my (the author of the Psalm) master אדני. There are not two words for "Lord" or God. Two divine beings are not involved. On the basis of the theme of the Psalm, clearly God's reassurance to David that his reign will be an enduring one, we can readily understand the simple wording of the Psalm. To read "Lord" for both יהוה and אדני is not to understand the profound difference of the two.

Perhaps it would help to consider how Spanish speaking people use the word *señor*. *El Señor* is God. Mr. Gomez is *Señor Gomez*.

Over time, traditional Jews would only say "Ah-do-shem" for God's specific name or simply "Ha-shem, The Name."

---

53 In the incident involving Moses and the burning bush, (Ex. 3:2-15) Moses asks to know God's name and is rebuffed. This reluctance to reveal the specific name of the God of the Hebrews is to be understood in terms of the Egyptian use of a god's name by a Priest is to compel him/her to do the bidding of the Priest, i.e., magic.

In the most recent translation of the Jewish scripture, the committee simply distinguished יהוה and אדני by calling the former "Lord" and the latter lord. This rendering also distinguishes between the divine and the human. Note the use of a capital "L" in one case and lower case "l" in the other.[54]

In spite of the complex debate, in this Psalm, the weight of the New Testament text is on the thrust that Jesus is the Messiah ben David.

---

54 Published by the Jewish Publication Society, Philadelphia, PA, 1985.

Chapter 12

The Allegory of Jonah and the Whale

The belief in a future resurrection for the faithful was a basic belief of the Pharisees and the masses of the Israelites long before the time of Jesus. The possibility of a resurrection was so prominent among the people (except for the Sadducees and their followers) that some of Jesus's immediate group (all Jews) thought he might be the resurrected John the Baptist or perhaps one of the resurrected prophets.

The details of the account of the resurrection of Jesus, as recorded in the New Testament, inevitably bring to mind the experience of Jonah as described in the book that bears his name in the Jewish scriptures. In that book we are told that Jonah was swallowed by a whale (i.e., he died) but was spit out (i.e., resurrected) on the third day.

The comparison between the story of the death and resurrection of Jesus follows the details of the Jonah story. The New Testament actually notes the comparison, that Jesus was resurrected "on the third day" like Jonah. The inference seems to be that this part of the tradition is a foretelling of what is to happen to Jesus. Again, we have an illustration that binds Jesus to his Jewish background.

Chapter 13

Anti-Jewish Sentiments in the New Testament

Some Jews have a negative view of the New Testament, because some of its narrative either seems to attack Jews or provides a base leading to hatred of the Jews.

Since almost all of the early followers of Jesus were Jews themselves, it seems that these negative passages must have been added quite late; perhaps when Christianity had become the official religion of the Roman Empire (4th Century C.E.).

In his work, "The Anguish of the Jews," Father Flannery points to the New Testament description of the crucifixion as the source of much anti-Semitism. The New Testament description of events leading up to the tragic death of Jesus clearly make the High Priest of the Jewish Temple a primary villain. Elsewhere in our book this author emphasizes the fact that the High Priest held his position only by Roman authority, but the New Testament author(s) of the story seem intent to lead guilt away from the infamous Pontius Pilate, the Roman. Further, a Jewish person is described as proclaiming, "The guilt be upon us and our people *forever!*" Now, what purpose would a Jew have in so involving future generations of his people?

The learned Christian might understand that the crucifixion was an essential part of the Christian religion and that the suffering and death of Jesus was a necessity in their doctrine of suffering and salvation. The average Christian, down through the centuries however, had difficulty grasping this profound fact. He knew only that "The Jews killed our Lord." Unfortunately this latter teaching has too often emanated from the Churches themselves.[55]

How wonderful it is that most Christians in the United States today have learned to overcome the earlier hatred of the Jews and have come to be our friends!

With the Catholic Church, for example, Pope John Paul the Second has made an heroic effort to uproot past ill feelings, and interfaith understanding and activities have increased over time.

Whether or not the New Testament has a few parts which are negative towards the Jews, this should not be a compelling reason for us Jews to reject the entire New Testament. It is still primarily a Jewish work, written primarily by Jews and has much to teach us about what some Jews believed and to what they aspired in that day and time.

In his new work, *Modern Jews Engage the New Testament*, Rabbi Dr. Michael J. Cook seems to reveal the "Gospel Dynamic," as he calls it. This dynamic, Dr. Cook declares, is primarily the contribution of later authors of the New Testament. To understand this "Dynamic," we have to understand that each author is strongly influenced by the historic times in which he lived. Jesus himself seems to have

---

55 See Father Edward H. Flannery's detailed work, *The Anguish of the Jews*, the MacMillan Company, New York, 1965, Paperback edition.

been motivated by the desperate times in which all Jews in that era lived under heavy Roman rule.

One of the reasons for Jewish avoidance of reading the New Testament today is the memory of Christian attempts to convert the Jews in the Middle Ages.[56] Moreover, many Jewish communities were often persecuted or actually killed, in large numbers by zealous Christians.

One of the worst periods for the Jews of Europe was the time of the Crusades, when Christian animosity towards the Arabs grew into hatred of all people who were not Christians. It was also not unusual for Jews to suffer as the result of bad economic times ("The Jews caused it") or during disasters of nature. The Jews were blamed for the bubonic plague. Ignorance and superstition often led to fictitious libels, i.e., ("the Jews make their unleavened bread for Passover with the blood of innocent Christian children"), etc.

---

56 [1] See Father Edward H. Flannery's detailed work, *The Anguish of the Jews*, the MacMillan Company, New York, 1965.

Chapter 14

A Curious Event in the Life of Jesus

The New Testament is full of teachings found in the Tanach (Old Testament) and many teachings found in the Talmud. One section of the Talmud is called "The Sayings of the Fathers." It consists primarily of teachings of the ancient Jewish sages collected in one brief collection. One such teaching is "the Sabbath is made for man" which implies that the rules of the Sabbath may be broken under extreme circumstances. Jesus quotes many of these sayings well known in the Jewish community, except that the teaching is altered slightly, i.e., "the Son of Man is Lord of the Sabbath"(Matthew 12:1-8). We have noted before that the Son of Man is a common expression in the Hebrew of that day meaning "a human being" (ben Adam) and is so used by the Prophet Ezekiel many times and with exactly that implication.

In later days, such as the time when the Book of Daniel was written, the phrase is used to indicate a special person ushering in the days of the Kingdom of God. The text reads "one like unto a ben Adam, a human being will be seen coming in the clouds…." To a group such as that headed by Jesus, this phrase would have apocalyptic implications. Thus, when Jesus uses the phrase "Son of Man" he may (or may not) intend it as a reference to the event described by Daniel. No matter how Jesus uses the phrase, it is found used in Jewish sources on different occasions.

What happens to Jesus (except for the Crucifixion), his Jewish background seems obvious.

There is another major exception in the New Testament. There is presented the Story of the Temptation of Jesus by the devil. In the story, the devil takes Jesus to a high place and says to Jesus, "Behold the glories of the world. All these things I will give thee, if thou wilt fall down and worship me." (Matt 4:8-9). Jesus replies with a thoroughly Jewish answer, quoting scripture, "it is written, 'Thou shalt worship the Lord thy God,' and Him only shalt Thou serve," (Matt 4:10). This idea is the essence of the key prayer in every Jewish Service (the *Sh'ma*). What is curious to a Jew about this New Testament story is not the reaction of Jesus but the fact that the devil appears as a deity in opposition to God. There is very little said about a devil in the Tanach (Old Testament). He appears as an angel in the Book of Job, and there he is only in the role of an accuser informing God that Job appears to be righteous only because God has been so good to him. If God will take away some of his good fortune and afflict Job personally, He will see how fickle Job's devotion is. As the Tanach story unfolds, God does test Job, and Job reacts by demanding that God confront him in a court of law to explain the justice in His actions. Most scholars believe the Book of Job to be a play in which the questions of the time are debated – why do the righteous suffer? Still the role of Satan ("the adversary") is only a relatively minor one. He certainly does not appear as a deity seeking worshippers.

The notion that Satan is a deity (eternally present) serving in a major capacity shows the influence of the Persian religious doctrine fostered by the prophet Zoroaster. Zoroaster taught that the world is a struggle between two deities, the God of Good and the God of Evil.

Judaism has contended that there is but one God responsible for good and evil, and He rewarded moral human actions with good and immoral human action with evil. The presence of evil in the world is explained by the battle within a person. Each of us has a *"yetzer ha-tov"* (the good inclination) and an inclination to do evil (*yetzer ha-ra*). Each of us must labor to see that our inclination for good dominates. To help us in this battle, God has given us the Torah, the laws of Moses. To follow the Torah is the path of life and peace; to disobey it is the path to turmoil and death. (See Deuteronomy, the Fifth Book of the Torah)

Both Jesus and Paul claimed to be strictly observant of the Torah and what Jesus emphasized in his teaching was the moral law of the Torah.

The Torah does not mention the devil. Such a notion emanated from folk customs as our people picked up beliefs of the non-Jews around them.

Jesus admonishes his disciples to follow even "the least of the commandments" in the Torah (Matt 5:18-19). It is Paul, who was anxious to bring non-Jews into the fold, who attempted to make it easy for them by de-emphasizing the rituals in the Torah and in the oral law.

Chapter 15

Should Jews Read the New Testament?

When Christians pay homage to Jesus, who lived about 2,000 years ago and whom most Christians call, "Lord," or "Son of God," we Jews often wonder why it is that so many non-Jews have selected this one Jew and made so much of him. For our part, we have regarded Jeremiah and Moses as being equally as great as or greater than Jesus, yet we have considered neither of them to be divine. Indeed, our scripture says that no person knows where Moses was interred, since it was not uncommon for people to worship at the spot where a truly great man was buried. Since Jews have always been taught that all humans are created in God's image, but one person cannot be God; since we have been taught that God cannot be pictured in human form or in any other form, we have shied away from a sympathetic understanding of Jesus. We have felt that to come close to him, even to examine him and what he stood for in his time, is to risk "*Hillul Ha-Shem* (profanation of God's name)." To examine Jesus closely has been a matter taboo for most Jews, lest they become guilty of committing some kind of heresy.

There is a great trend in Christianity today whereby more and more Christians feel that to understand their faith more clearly, they must turn to the study of ancient Judaism. There is clearly in Christian circles today a great thirst for understanding Judaism in all of its dimensions, and especially, in those dimensions which go into the make-up of Jesus. Should we Jews merely sit passively by while Christians commendably try to learn something about our faith? Shouldn't we try to learn something about our faith, too, and one of the best ways to learn about the Judaism of 2,000 years ago is to read the New Testament. In spite of the fact that the New Testament seems to Jews to be written with a partisan viewpoint; in spite of the fact that later contributors to its pages reflect an anti-Jewish bias, no Jew can read the teachings of Jesus without noting its substantially Jewish perspective and emphasis. If one knows anything about the Talmud, that compendium of Jewish laws and knowledge prepared several centuries before and after the birth of Jesus, one can see that Jesus spoke, for the most part, as some of the rabbinical teachers of his day.[57] It seems he was trying to sift through the growing volume of ritual in order to arrive at the basic heart of Judaism, even as Rabbi Hillel had done fifty years before Jesus and as the Hebrew Prophet Jeremiah had done 600 years before Hillel.

In short, except for a few pages added to the New Testament by comparatively late authors and editors, the New Testament appears as a Jewish book, written by Jews, concerning matters that happened to Jews, and presenting moral and ethical teachings from the Jewish tradition. To be sure, there are certain viewpoints in the New Testament

---

57 See *The Jewish Sources of the Sermon on The Mount*, Gerald Friedlander, KTAV Publishing House, Inc. New York, 1911, 1969. Dr. Friedlander demonstrates the Jewish Soures of most of Jesus' teachings.

which are inconsistent with our bible (Tanach) and with mainstream Judaism, but there are other books written by Jews which represent divergent viewpoints, and we do not hesitate to read these books. Some such books, for example, have been preserved in a collection known as the Apocrypha, and we would not even have this collection if the Catholic Church had not preserved it as part of their Holy Bible.[58] Even though we might feel that the perspective of some of these apocryphal books is outside the ken of normative Judaism, we read these books, from time to time, just to learn what some Jews believed 2200 years ago, just to learn what their problems were and how they attempted to solve them. By reading the apocryphal books and noting that the Rabbis of that day outlawed them as inconsistent with normative Judaism, just in this way do we learn all the more clearly what normative Judaism was at that time. If we read the New Testament, we discover why the Rabbis could not accept it as scripture.

Most Jews of today cannot accept the New Testament doctrine of the cataclysmic end to history, because ours is a religion for this world and within human history as we know it. The New Testament has a doctrine of salvation by faith, through believing that Jesus was a dying and rising God. The concept of a God of agriculture who dies in winter and is re-born in springtime is one of the oldest themes of ancient Semitic religions. The founders of Judaism taught that God was the creator of nature, but He was not *in* nature. That is, he did not die, like the things in nature, so there was no need for Him to be resurrected. The doctrine of the dying and resurrected God is alien to normative Judaism which teaches that salvation comes in this world in normal human society, as people strive to make that society more just and peaceful. The New Testament has a doctrine that humans are forgiven

---

[58] The Christian Bible consists of both Old and New Testament.

for their sins through the sacrifice of the "first born son of God," that is, Jesus. This is alien to prophetic Judaism which turned against the priestly notion of vicarious atonement and substitute sacrifice. On the contrary, Judaism developed, through the Prophets, the idea that each person must save himself through his own deeds.[59]

More and more Christian scholars, as well as Jewish scholars, contend that many of these New Testament notions which are alien to normative Judaism were alien also to Jesus. More and more we learn that it was Paul, who never saw Jesus, and others, who introduced many non-Jewish ideas into the recreated meaning of the deceased Jesus. It has even been suggested by some Christian teachers that if Jesus were to return to earth today, he would belong to the synagogue, as he did in his own time.

Julius Wellhausen, the great Christian biblical scholar, wrote in 1905, "Jesus was not a Christian, he was a Jew." Dr. Wellhausen, whose works on the bible are known to every bible scholar, wrote further, "[Jesus]… did not preach a new faith but taught people to do the will of God, and in his opinion, as also in the opinion of the Jews, that will of God was to be found in the law of Moses and in the other books of (Jewish) scripture" (Einleitung In Die Drei Ersten Evangelein), parentheses this author's.

Harry Emerson Fosdick, the celebrated Pastor of New York's Riverside Church for many years, has stated, "The Church has garbed the simple Jewish teacher beyond all recognition in heavy brocaded garments of sterile theology, until the real Jesus has been got rid of altogether." Perhaps, we have been intuitively wise in standing four square against the Pauline presentation of Jesus. But need we be so opposed to the real Jesus, as Fosdick says, "the gentle Jew," perhaps

---

[59] Ezekiel and Jeremiah.

one of history's outstanding teachers?

Dr. Lynn Abbott, the Christian theologian, writing in his book *What Christianity Means To Me*, has said,

> But when I came to study the teachings of Jesus… I found that he never mentioned vicarious atonement, or the fall of Adam, nor the trinity… nor did I find in Christ's teaching any provision of a new theology or a new ecclesiastical system to take the place of the old. Born a Jew, he remained a Jew to the day of his death… The notion that Jesus organized a Christian Church to take the place of the decaying Jewish Church has very little evidence to support it…. The institutions of Christianity, however important they may be, were not framed by Christ and imposed on his followers. They were gradually developed by his followers after his death…. Christianity converted paganism, but paganism changed Christianity.

What Dr. Abbott is clearly saying is that the religion *of* Jesus was far different from the religion that grew up *about* Jesus.

What are the true teachings of Jesus, if he did not teach any of the mystic sacraments about himself? The answer to this question is given in the New Testament in a little incident where Jesus is asked, "Master, which is the great commandment in the law?" Jesus answers, "You shall love the Lord your God with all your heart with all your soul and all your mind, and you shall love your neighbor as yourself."[60]

---

[60] Matthew 22:36-39 RSV, compare 19:16ff where the question is, "What good must I do to have eternal life?" Jesus answers, "if you would enter life, keep the commandments." Jesus names five of the Ten Commandments plus the command to love your neighbor. These are the so-called "Noahidic laws" which under Jewish tradition are all that are required to the non-Jew. According to Jewish tradition, the Jew, in addition, must observe the other commandments relating to God. This may be the inference of 19:17-19.

This is the essence of the teaching of Jesus. You will observe, of course, that the first of these statements is in The Jewish prayer book, and it comes from the fifth book of our scripture, Deuteronomy (6:4-5). The second statement, concerning love of neighbor, comes from our book of Leviticus (19:18). In brief, Jesus readily quoted Jewish scripture in summarizing his view of life. In fact, if one reads the 19th chapter of the book of Leviticus, one will find almost all of the ethical teachings of Jesus including the teaching of concern for one's enemy.

In our brief book, we can only introduce this important subject, but we can at least project this point. Jesus is rather typical of the Jewish people in a very profound sense, for he was crucified, murdered, if you will, by non-Jews who for some reason could not tolerate his doctrine of a revolutionary world in which all people would be brothers and sisters and tyrants would be overthrown. While some Christians still cling to the notion that the "Jews" are responsible for the death of Jesus, the fact remains that the Romans killed him for daring to assert a claim to the throne of ancient Judea. To be the Messiah, one had to be king of an independent Judea. This is why the Romans mocked him by writing across his cross, "Jesus of Nazareth, King of the Jews": This is why they mocked him by garbing him in purple robes, purple being the symbol of royalty. This is why they gave him a crown, to be sure, a crown of thorns.[61] For this he was killed, as Rabbi Akiba was killed, as Jews throughout history have been crucified, and maimed, and cremated, and butchered. Jesus was only one of millions of Jews who were unjustly killed, but since he was killed, he, like all the other Jewish martyrs, is a symbol of what the world has done to the Jew, as well as to other victims of prejudice and misunderstanding, like Martin Luther King, or, indeed, like many Christians.

---

61 Matthew 27:27-29.

The saintly Rabbi Leo Baeck condemned to a concentration camp, but whose spirit Hitler could not conquer, has written, "... The Gospel, which was originally something Jewish, becomes a book... within Jewish literature.... It is a Jewish book because... the pure air of which it is full and which it breathes is that of the Jewish Holy Scriptures; because a Jewish spirit and none other lives in it; because Jewish faith and Jewish hope, Jewish suffering and Jewish distress, Jewish knowledge and Jewish expectations, and these alone resound through it...." Dr. Baeck concludes, "Judaism may not pass it by, nor wish to give it up."[62]

Perhaps the time will never come when Jews will want to give the New Testament status equal to that of the Old Testament, but if we want to understand a significant segment of Jewish history, Jews ought to read the New Testament, and if we want to understand the individual Jew through whom Jewish ethics came to a large portion of the world, we have to come to know the man Jesus.[63]

---

[62] Leo Baeck, *Judaism and Christianity – The Gospel as a Document of History.*

[63] A much more thorough work on this general theme is to be found in chapter ten of *Can Faith Survive*, Dr. Maurice N. Eisendrath, published by McGraw-Hill, New York, 1964. I am indebted to Dr. Eisendrath for some of the quotations here included.

Glossary

Hellenism – The name given to the Greek culture which was imposed on every land the Greeks conquered.

Leprosy – A common disease of the biblical period which included skin blemishes.

Literary Prophets – Prophets with a Biblical book bearing their name.

Pseudepigrapha – Name given to those books written by Jews but not officially included in the canon but professing to be biblical in character.

Tanach – Hebrew word for the Hebrew Scriptures (Old Testament).

Zealots – A group in Jewish society of those advocating more extreme tactics in resisting the Romans.

Bibliography

Baeck, Leo. *Judaism and Christianity – The Gospel as a Document of History*.

Baumgard, Rabbi Herbert M. D.H.L. "*The Meaning of the Hebrew Word 'TOV' in the Scripture,*" Library, Hebrew Union College, Jewish Institute of Religion, New York, NY.

Blenkinsopp, Joseph. *A History of Prophecy in Israel*, Westminster John Knox Press, Louisville, KY.

Cook, Rabbi Dr. Michael J. *Modern Jews Engage the New Testament*, The Jewish Publication Society of America, Philadelphia, PA, 2008.

Eisendrath, Rabbi Dr. Maurice M. *Can Faith Survive*, McGraw Hill, NY 1964.

Friedlander, Gerald. *The Jewish Source of the Sermon on the Mount*, KTAV Publishing, Hoboken, NJ, 1911.

Grant, Dr. F.C. *Ancient Judaism and the New Testament*, MacMillan Co., NY.

Greenstone, Julius H. *The Messiah Idea in Jewish History*, Jewish Publication Society of America, Philadelphia, PA, 1943 (reprint).

Flannery, Father Edward H. *The Anguish of the Jews*,

MacMillan Company, New York, NY, 1965 (paperback edition).

Klausner, Dr. Joseph. *Jesus of Nazareth*, MacMillan Company, 1925.

Moore, G.F. *Judaism*, Vol. 1, 6th Impression, Harvard University Press, Cambridge, MA, 1950.

Moore, G.F. *Judaism*, Vol. 2, Harvard University Press, Cambridge, MA.

Moore, G.F. *History of Religions*, Revised Edition. Scribner and Sons, NY, 1946.

Orlinsky, Dr. Harry M. *Essays in Biblical Culture and Bible Foundation*, KTAV Publishing House, Inc., NY, 1974.

Zeitlin, Solomon. *Who Crucified Jesus?*, Second Edition, Harper, NY, 1947.

Biblical Archeological Review, September 1, October, 2008, Vol. 3, Number 5, "The Messiah Son of Joseph."

The Holy Bible, Authorized Version, ed. Rev. C. Schofield, New and Improved Edition, Oxford University Press, NY, 1917.

The Holy Bible, the Revised Standard Version, T. Nelson and Sons, NY, 1953 p. 36.

The Holy Bible, Revised Standard Version, The World Publishing Company, Cleveland, OH, and New York, NY.

The Prophets: A New Translation of the Holy Scriptures According to the Masoretic Text. The Jewish Publication Society of America, Philadelphia, PA, 1978.